AF322705

POETRY IS MOTION:
MIND, BODY & SOUL

POETRY IS MOTION:
MIND, BODY & SOUL

VIRAL GOR

EP
HOUSE

First paperback edition - April 2023
Paperback ISBN: 978-1-0881-2592-2
Hardcover ISBN: 979-8-8692-8289-7
Digital ISBN: 979-8-8689-2645-7

PRINTED IN THE UNITED STATES OF AMERICA ON ACID-FREE PAPER

TABLE OF CONTENTS

PART 1: FAMILY

Guns and Roses

The pain I seen through my mother's eyes couldn't be
controlled by these other guys.
To my surprise, I rose up above all the disclaimers.
I kept it in straight line, middle fingers.
They couldn't grow, surpass what they tried to know, but it
was all me.
I didn't show, off is what they wanted to see and I've been
doing me since I've became me.
So, understand this, I have held my own since I was three,
observing what was surrounding me.

My mom asked me, "Will you ever change?"
I ignored what she was preaching to me but, she was trying
to make me a better me.
Being blinded by the rage, money, and games, I brushed it
off, acting like I wasn't that soft.
After all the struggle, I still got no fans.
I thought I was the main man until I realized, I was torn
between a hood and a cave man.

I figured it out.
What I was tripping about was unnecessary, stressing
myself out.
Couldn't understand why it seemed so scary yet, was seen
as so merry.
Great fate, I hate, and I still participated.
It's a shame, a lackluster life of he.
He, which cannot be contained until I tame me.
In essence, I can't see through he.
He, which is I, cannot see, until I, be within reach of the
achievements I plan to reach.

A Rock & A Hard Place

I'm trying to take both sides as if I'm not trying to lose a friend.
I won't speak on the trouble about being recognized as the
one that's got to decide what happens from here 'til the
end.
I sent out well wishes and stayed neutral.
But got backlash from both sides, it was brutal.
No doodle but the drawings on the wall.
A rock and a hard place, something I did not want to call.

Bloodline

We got good genes in our family.
Holding it down, this isn't insanity.
This is vanity, no wait, that's fair.
Let's think about this right here.
Think about the times each one of them struggled to get to
their careers.
Until they got to the place where they can hold their head
high and say, "I survived."
Think about the struggles they went through to strive high.
The benefits of struggle are real, they ended up eating well
with hot meals.
Delicious, as their taste for success, was harder than steel.
Let's keep on this roll, steady pacing as the wheel stayed
stable.
Denying all distractions with vigor and zeal.
This is our canvas, let's paint our shield.

Discovery

With every kiss and hug, I catch that bug that won't fade
away.
Every time I see that face, the whispers shout loud,
"That's the one beyond infinite days."
Just as records play, the melodies of our harmonies
synchronize, forever stay.
Could this be love?
Passion, desire like earth, exploding through the volcanic
energy that sores higher.
Deep thoughts between reality and fantasy, am I insane?
I forgot how the world looks without her grace.
Clarity is focused as an eye test.
I can never rest knowing you are far away.
I will search the seven seas and four corners of the earth as they
say.
A sense of relief as I grab your hand and hold on tight.
You are my one and only sign, like neon lights.

Maturity

Remember those days you had as a child?
Trying to fly that kite in the daylight while, breathing in
fresh air.
Thinking about nothing but playing right here.
We dreamt of going higher, perhaps flying, soaring while
others stare.
Those heights we wanted to reach became something of a
distant memory.
To those that got told to settle down and the rest will be
up to luck like winning the lottery.
We gasped at the sight of adulthood before saying it's all
good.
We were living stress free but had to grow up quick, no
Sesame Street.

Uncle Sam, not Toucan, damn.
We wanted to strive and achieve but as a child, what do
you do when things stop, you grieve.
Running through the playground enjoying the sounds, no
frowns.
All we felt was upbeat not to retreat, but to trick was our
treat, as Halloween came around, we suddenly got plenty
to eat.
Nowadays, we fight that rat race to get a seat.
Beat ourselves so bad, migraines sneak up on us like it was
from the heat.
Really?
Is that why we grew up so fast?
So, we can get our 9 to 5?
That's why we had to pass that class?

Family Man

The feeling was intense.
I squeezed my head and thought in the past sense.
I should've protected myself some more.
But low and behold, the good swimmer didn't miss her
mark.
I'm here sitting, waiting to fill up this empty cart.
My unstable ways have to end.
I can't stop reminiscing on the things I wanted to send.
This is the beginning of the end.
My life is now in a different lane, listen up my friend.
Put all extras aside, focus on the star that is seen within
your eyes.
My little twinkle toes has no foes, only a father that is
proud to have a daughter.
A man stands up for his family to eat.
Kickstart from the mark that gets settled with no defeat.
The craziness is parted once my other half smirked, no
streak.
No leaks here, I fuel this fire to burn everywhere as I
become a different man and all my goals are zoned into
one thing.
I am a family man.
It's true, it's beneficial, but don't let it overtake you.
There's much more to it and that's the truth.
Becoming content consumes you through.
Maturity goes beyond the numbers;
it's how one cultivates manners and growth through
countless suppers.
Reaction is significant, no need for buffers.

Our Unborn Dream

I don't know what life could've been had we had you.
One thing is for certain, that we almost had you.
We would've been happier because we would've made sure
everything was perfect.
Baby girl or boy, whatever it would've been, you would've
had two people try to define everything they were in.
We would've tried to estimate and regulate life so subtle, to
a point where you could live free and get out of that small
bubble.
This is a cradle, but we did not want to rob you.
We wanted to give you, life experiences, which we wanted
to.
Unfortunately, we took the wrong turn and you went
under.
The future is not the past, let's make another.
I would want us to get back together and have you.
Our beautiful unborn, smile baby, we're about to have
two.

Air-Walker

This day and age, I look to my family and friends so they
can benefit me in every way.
But that's a two-way road and I'm gonna help as much as I
can, I'm not going to fold.
We are bold and getting older.
Therefore, we have to stop fighting and improve the odor.
It's the New World Order.
Persuaded and steered.
Clever, not feared.
Remember this clear, this is the goal of my mind that I
commandeered.
Hijacking like I'm packing this seat.
Riding in the streets, pulling out all stops, like signs to
read.
Directions and drive.
Shift the gear, hauling weight from within the inside.
Propel is the objective, it isn't to hide.
Straight up, let's simply fly.

In Memoriam

Death waits for no one, and serves his time.
As if one last breath could be heard like a chime.
The cries could be heard miles away.
Today is a new day.
Do not cry uncontrollably at the fact that he or she is
gone.
But celebrate their life that was filled with so much.
They will be again, just in a new form.
Smiling down on you and watching over.
The soul will never be lost, just that their body has been
covered over.
Think about the good times you've shared.
Playing every memory in your mind like a projector.
Sitting down staring into the distant air into a sector.
Only you can see your relationship goes deeper.
Those thoughts are beyond a keeper.
Just know you have tried your very hardest and they
appreciated you more than you'll ever know.
May they Rest in Peace and protect your soul.

Diwali

The festival of lights celebrated with family.
The motivations and aspirations are our philosophy.
Sal Mubarak to all.
Passion, respect is the foundation, no fall.
Dating back hundreds of years to today.
The present is always a challenge but in a good way.
Thank you Bhagwan for all that is today.
We join at functions to celebrate together.
Family feasts, drinking, sharing laughs as we smile and
treat each other with joy.
Darkness overtaken by the light that we share.
We light diyas and pray.
Cracking coconuts on the footsteps of our homes.
With belief that our good hearts will take over evil any day.
I constantly pray that everyone here will succeed in every
way.
Hope over despair, celebrating new beginnings.
This is the time to look at those closest to you and share
faith.
Always walk with your head held high as we guide the light
to gather and say,
Happy Diwali to all and to all a good day.

PART II: RELATIONSHIPS

Culture

My culture is free, however, there are vultures inside that
try and be.
While you try to succeed, they suck the life out of all those
who are trying to breathe.
I see the seeds and many plead, but not the fifth.
They keep talking non-stop like a gossip column, hanging
on the rack, waiting to get picked.
So much jealousy and envy within our own kind and I just
don't get it, we need to rewind.
Back to the times, when all we had, was our clan and pride.

See, all the other cultures rise, as one unit stands above, no
guns.
Wanna be gangsters and tough guys, so many things I've
seen that I continually despise.
That's why I strayed a bit, to get some clarity and try
staying fit.
Brain exercises that made me think that I'm here standing,
not going to sink.
But my observation left a bad stink.
Brown people hating on each other as if we're all rocking
pink.
Now the reservations cancelled, we can't even sit.

What a pity, this is not what I wanted to see within our
community.
We should be united, but as back stabbers come, like Julius
Caesar we've found out who really is scum.

Too prideful like Leonidas but lacking 300 to charge the
mount, it's so different if one comes out and runs all
others out.
It's not about what makes you a man; it's the journey and
how many hands you help rise as a band.
But understand we're trying to be all that we can be.
I'm helping all others on the way to the top as much as I can
believe.
Anything we want, we got to strive for, and the culture is
golden in rock form.
I fight for shattering glass ceilings regardless if it's
corporate bull, it's fan stealing.
I mean why?

Let's just say we need to be unified.
And what we need for our culture is not to be
dehumanized.
Pride plus growth equals hope.
Our culture needs to continue to grow as a whole.
Our culture is too bold.

Co-op

Why are we fighting?
You are lightening, furious, thunderous & full of energy.
I am the grass of delicacy.
Reluctantly, trying to ease the tension through credibility.
Sensing the calm before the storm.
Preparing for the inevitable.
I am susceptible to the results of your actions.
Yet, I stay.
Waiting for the moment the rays shine through those
vicious clouds to get back to that place.
Where, we are one, as light and day.
Bright side like follow my page.
This is the way.
Getting past the craze and never raining away.
Select your mind state.
Let's cooperate.

Focus

Embraced each other as if we were meant to lose.
We lost each other, but never let go.
Walked the trenches of rock, dirt, and sand to get to the
turf.
The lights got closer, but we got further.
Scary sight as we tried to fight an uphill battle.
No cattle to feed off, we're against that, but had to figure
out our plan fast.
The darkness set in and cold wind blew.
The rain started drizzling and my internal flame grew.
I will not let us lie on this dirt.
I will not let this girl feel hurt.
I will not leave until we are safe.
I got us, that's a promise I intended to keep, forever
placed.
As the cars got smaller, we set in motion.
Our journey across barren waste lands, where, times were
tougher.
No buffer but we were angry and lit.
Tried to help but got irritated as we both wanted to walk
in a different direction to find grace.
We heard the ocean waves thrash the black sand.
We saw a few hands take shelter in an abandoned plane
crash.
30 minutes later, we arrived after a 40-minute journey that
was not visualized from the start.
We walked separately until we reached this site but battled
all the way like a dog and cat fight.
Despite our efforts, we refuted, angrily answering
questions, driving two hours from our stay.

(continued)

We snarled and prayed on each other's emotions.
What a sad day!
However, the past ruins the future if you let it.
Don't bring it forward until you found peace in the face
that it's dead.
Enjoy with the one you're with and leave the past behind
you as if I didn't make a difference with your most recent
shift.
Love, care, emotion.
Emphasizing these things, sometimes causes commotion
and misfortune.
If you have the world in front of you, don't bring forward
something that will come over you.
It's good to know sorrow, but better to find peace in the
days of tomorrow.
Especially with who you're with, cause let's be honest, life's
a bitch.

Colours

How do you know when it's time to call the curtains?
It's when it's clear, for certain.
But these emotions left over could be misconstrued as a
burden.
A beautiful ship that casted its way.
As the distance grew from the shores, lightening stuck and
we heard the roars.
Determined to avoid sinking, we fought through.
Evidently, it was also the reason anger brewed.
While we worked together, everything seemed to come off
as rude.
This was our view.
Didn't want to abandon ship, but we both knew.
Only time will tell how far we've come to survive what was
once, a beautiful hue.

Depth Chart

Was it I?
What did I do to make these blues dive to the level of the sea?
Below depth, the heart got drenched.
Soaked until death was seen.
Catastrophic, the stomach tightens and doesn't let loose.
Tried to get away, but the noose was too tight.
Sad, I was trying to reach glad with you.
But sadly, we couldn't overcome so we simply grew.
Far apart.
I guess we both needed the restart.
I didn't, but was forced once you kept your distance and shook.
I was quick to look and got booked.
You closed the chapter on our book.
Goodbye.

Price

It's funny how life goes in full circle.

Karma is seen, overflowed.

Coming back around like "oh, you didn't know?"

I glow with the joy and privilege of seeing wrong moves

turn out to be the right choices.

Reflection of self and what was desired.

Right moves ahead? I thought more liars.

I walk through fire and go to the Oceanic Sea.

Saw the calm relaxing waves sliding up to the shores, felt

like I needed to plea.

You came right back, and I waved goodbye like I told you,

you'd see.

Go on and experience some more hardships.

Once you've realized what you had, this ship has sailed.

All you can do is gaze and wonder why.

Why the betrayal? Why did it fail?

Simple as can be, you lost sight and had to read braille.

You didn't want to converse on good terms so that was

the reason we went stale.

I've crossed the trenches and jumped up with my shield.

Knocked each shot down as I played the field.

I kept my head held high.

The price of playing was revealed.

One Time Friends

Thought it was clear back in the days when as a child we
did everything in infinite ways.
How foolish I was to think it would last 'til today.
Things change, people turn, 180 and then I yearn.
Cringing at my poor foresight.
Forgetting to weather the storm like everything was alright.
Bright, not what I am.
I thought I had real friends, until I decided to stay silent
for more then I really can.

Then I saw the sad truth, the people you held down forget
you.
Step 2, push past or stand up, let your thoughts be heard,
not bagged up.
Or else, that top will pop as you cram up.
Listen to the words so they don't get jammed up.

Little circles or bigger ones, you decide where you're from.
But keep in mind, the line to get to the one you really
share your time with.
But they side eye you like they don't know what you've
gone through or what's going on.
How can they be helpful when they're the ones holding
you from achieving stars beyond?

Tough Love

We try to toughen up like we're all born rangers.
Protecting our loved ones from real danger.
We all want to have things go smoothly like we're arrangers.
But that's not reality.
Things go astray as many of us, sit and wait.
The confidence gets built up then smashed down.
As if our hands weren't enough to put the trash down.
All smiles one day then followed up by a frown.
Even after taking her around town, she still got the nerve
to say,
"What are you doing to keep me regardless of this crown?"
As if I must convince her, this isn't a great sales pitch to
me either.
This is a mutual interview, don't get it confused.
We're both feeling each other out, unused.
Let's stop and just talk.
The intellectual mindset will make or break this.
Those are the clues.

Enjoyment

Happiness causes stress relief for the very people who let
themselves feel this peace and let them win over defeat.
It's going to be a show, kind of discreet.
Still showing the haters the heels of my feet.
They're behind in this race.
Trying to catch up to me is like the coyote trying to catch
up to the roadrunner for first place.
Turn around the sorrow and relive the days that kept you
feeling at ease with the things that are harmonious in life
and never feeling like your happiness is borrowed.
Don't think of the past, think about the now and leave the
future.
Your days are going by fast.
Staying in the past makes things weary and you'll never get
away from these things, they turn scary.
Overthinking situations causes ruckus, ruining
relationships, causing many to feel confused.
Things back then should be left back then and not let it
move forward with you or else you're going to strain your
days or whoever you're trying to pursue.
It can be misconstrued.
A new life is every day.
The man in the mirror is showing how you live today.
Look at the present as if it's a gift.
God sent down the angels and gave you a kiss.
Blessed to be around and whoever is with you in
happiness, to bring you up not down.

Keep the truth and understand my focused game, it's a
ferocious thing.
Truth be told, I've grown kind of old, but still young and
feel the pain this deep from the go on the run.
On to the next one as you try to forget, but certain
memories will never fade, like burns from a cigarette.
No shade, reenergize and make sure your next move
electrifies or rides out slow.
Never dipping down like salsa and chips below.
No flips but strive 'til you arrive to your main ship whether
it be colossal or coastal.
Don't hesitate; it's going to get emotional.

Share My World

Strolling through my mind and gazing at the wonders.
Of all that encompasses like times through thunder.
Lightning strike fast imagery, vivid as the day you see while
feeling that scorching heat.
1000 times over as you walk down the path of our soul;
counting down from infinity.
As you put on my sweater and enter my world, I would
like to show you how it unfolds as you walk through
searching for gold.
This lucky charm can't be sold, only found through your
own desires and will.
Finding this person will be its own thrill.
Share my world and let us walk around this big clock that
will never lock, but cherish our memories.
Playing one scene at a time as a painting.
What do we both get from this? What are we gaining?
Becoming one.

PART III: SELF-REFLECTION

I'm Inadequate

Hope beyond that of my dreams, I am inadequate.
Passion is just a wave passing by toward the drains, I'm
inadequate.
Perception of my image is factual, I'm inadequate.
Righteous mind but no action, I'm inadequate.
What the world sees is nothing compared to how you
drive.
Whether it's stick or automatic, the propulsion is firing sky
high.
If I am inadequate, it is because I have thought of all
outcomes.
I see myself in bliss like leaves sailing through the breeze.
I am inadequate?
No, sorry, I cannot lie because I am beyond adequate, I am
wise.
I am beyond adequate.
I have passion and continue to strive.
I am beyond adequate because I seek and give hope as we
all will rise.
We are not inadequate.
We are more than what meets the eye.

My Quest

I've loved and I've lost.
I came to the crossroads and looked at all the avenues.
I had to choose one, to cruise at the altitude, where I
didn't want to get bruised.
But I got hit harder than ever before.
I saw the eyes look at me and burrowed a hole in my soul.
Folded up like a lawn chair, I was stuck in the shed.
No light, but cracks exposed like infrared.
Sometimes, it's harder to face reality.
When something sucks the life out of you, it's a tragedy.
But it's up to your mind, body and soul to overcome
obstacles like Ms. Congeniality.
Move past the anxiety.
Face these issues head on and use variety.
Forget high society, think repair shop, full stop.
You will never lose when they eavesdrop.
You have their attention.
They want to see more.
You have your plan in motion that is devotion.
Their obsession in you is secure.
Let them watch with envy, give them the grand tour.
The verdict is out, you are an Entrepreneur.

I Rise

In happiness, we glow and start to wonder.
How things come to light from the darkness blunders.
The forces that be, try to hold us down.
But we will prevail as we rise beneath the ground.
The sky lights up as we walk and search.
The unidentified mindset that was unheard.
We conjure passion and hype until we seek that elevation.
To reach triumph, staying up all night.
None shall have our desires and will.
We will rise in a moment when our stars begin to seek
their thrills.

Planted

Saw fresh soil so I planted my seed.
I wanted to grow tall through sunshine as I feed.
I meant to soak in water through all my leaves.
Food for my roots as they are my sleeves.
I try to mount this ground right.
The secret is putting up a good fight.
All light, no darkness.
As my years age, I prepare for my inevitable decay.
How I counter that, through vigor and play.
My lungs are fresher than the day I was born.
This is my time.
I am beyond a thorn.

Poem of the First

Our night, listen to the stars, they radiate light.
Making us see the vision as clear as the eyes we had as a child,
moving towards and winning the fight.
Peep the mind, soul so divine and freshest ever, like the
first time we stole pears bike riding, no fairs.
See, we all seem to care, I swear.
I don't pay attention to negative individuals who try to
downshift the journey.
Watch close while I stunt so hard, they adore me.
Mi amor, don't wait to see me more.
No lie detection; I'm straight like no simulation, it's fate.
Patience is what they say, who is they as I lay.
Down for success, manifesting the goals, I don't digress.
I'm here soaking it all in, I digest.
Trying to be the best me, no pest.
I pay no mind to those who are inclined to lift weight like
a plate and show no triceps.
Weak, no push through.
Focus on what's beneficial, not official.
Forget the title, no wave necessary.
I swam in the oceans, fish cemeteries.
No ceremony for the glory, don't wait till you're 40.
Enjoy and grind as your mind uncovered your story.
Circumstances that had suddenly grew, there were just a
few.
Do you want to be known for causing ruckus or hitting
two?
Perhaps, you prefer brain dead work like zombies are
living proof.
Food for thought.

Pride

We have all been bullied one way or another.
Whether you were the cause, the reaction, the opposites or
other.
Listen here and remain calm, unlike mother.
Brother, sister or kids, we need to stick together as if unity
is all for one and one for all.
Strength in numbers and resources to help.
No bully will have their way with the assistance of self.

Hope Springs

Don't ever let anyone knock your hustle.
They don't know what you have been through.
They don't see your muscles.
Flexed and pulled in all directions.
Stability is the intention, but all they see is the final
product without hesitation.
You are your own inspiration.
Taken in strides to no avail.
Sail to your destination and plant your flag.
You have captured what you intended,
Forget the jet lag.

Redemption

Don't be afraid of failure, it helps you grow.
The passion should be fixed like no variables needed to go.
This is a continuous flow, ever going like waves in the
ocean starting millions of years ago.
These are opportunities to get better over time, you will
shine.
Try, try and try some more.
You will lose once you give up and try to cushion the
blow.
Embrace that setback to enforce a greater comeback.
Set your mindset past the lows.
This will be your life's soundtrack, listen to know.
Each track gives you lessons as you will be one step closer
to your goals.
Dreams that become reality, picture the show.
Over time, you will get better, you will get stronger.
Discourage the negativity that causes vertigo.
This isn't a game show, you're on your stage, get the
memo.
It reads, moves past the barriers to lift with gusto.
Lock in, load up and calibrate the ammo.
Your aim is to move past the range and hit your target that
may be hidden like camo.
Is your goal to get that Lambo?
Is your goal to get a better handle?
Is your goal to get past your past scandals?
It can all be achieved, as long as you stay consistent
amongst the resistance that wants you to bleed.
So, I plead, each failure comes with a success story.
Can we agree?
Your passion is the common denomination that you will
need to continuously feed.
Water your seed and watch the fruits of your labour,
blossom and live free.

Rise

Woke up on Mount Mackay.
Overlooked the cliff and saw what I thought was a maze
but was the city landscape.
Mesmerized by the site, I took a deep breath and left.
Couldn't believe what I witnessed beyond a few dozen that
were committed.
As the river stream runs downward, I dive in a spiral
thinking about my many rivals that fuel this bonfire.
No desire but was challenged by the hikers who did not
drift.

No phones, just you and nature.
Look within yourself to climb and hook like hangers.
Forget the dirt to get through.
Withstand the barrage of rocks falling towards you.
Your mission is to fight through and defeat the climb that
has at many times, defeated you.

A billion stars looking like diamonds in the night sky at the
top of that peak.
Wake that sleeping giant by making a gigantic shift and
leap.
Shaking the ground like an earthquake sneak.
Once that obstacle has been overtaken, no more leaks.
The rise to the top is the one which we will all need to
reach.
Let us Succeed.

Self-Reflection

You ever walk into a room so nice and the words just flow
and glide like you're skating on ice.
This is life.
The depth and science will tell us the physics in the air
tonight.
As we flare, we see the sparks move in all directions.
And those far, far away, unaware that they just witnessed
something, they can't stop but stare.
Is it rare? That's up to you.
As common as you want to get recognized for the thing
that you want to do.
Well things might change, grab you by your ankles and pull
you astray.
As you get crossed don't ever lose your way, don't get lost.
Enjoy the sights and sounds you are so eager to lose but at
what cost?
I see things change like new furniture, Chester.
But keep your head up and move past those jesters.
No time for foolishness and clowns.
We are on a mission.
The moon is in our grasp now.

Shining

You're born, you live, and you die.
Are you really living or just getting by?
Are you living life to the fullest or watching it pass right
by?
Sigh, but not for relief.
To think that you haven't been able to settle that craving
beneath.
The tooth aches something like wisdom seeks.
But peak in emotion as these emotions start feeling like
commotion.
Within your own mind and you're trying to prevent it from
cutting right by.
Pie, that won't settle your craving.
This is your free will but until you figure out what you
desire, the needs will never feel fulfilled.
Take it one step at a time, but know yourself as much as
time flies by.
Don't cry but cherish the fruits of your labour.
It may seem as if things aren't going your way, but patience
is the key ingredient, flavor.
Don't sign the waiver and allow yourself to be fooled.
No rushing in like how Chandler grew.
This is your view, beautiful as only you know what you
went through.
Shout out to all those who pulled, they knew.
Time is of the essence and the journey is your own.
Find a companion on the way and those cheap thrills turn
into an adventure like building up a home.
This is a part of it like it's in the genome.
DNA spread across the globe and one thing uncovered.
We are destined for something.
Shining on our own.

Social Cast

How are we all so connected, yet disconnected more than
ever before?
We have all been affected whether you are conscious or
not.
This has gone above, beyond the top.
The emotionless net.
Yet, we are always prying, trying to see what others are
doing.
Unfortunately, all you're consuming are the social
platforms that reveals the best life.
Missing the realism of most lives.
Stay woke as those conversations rise.

Strength

I stand on my own.
Embracing the gusty winds that whistle and blow.
I flow, aside from my hair.
I aspire to be the centerpiece I declare.
Goodness me.
Let me rock my shades and protect myself from the cloudy
influences that say,
"She doesn't have what it takes."
Let me prove you wrong and keep striving.
I'm driving through this hate.
I penetrate the eternal eclipse that resides over home plate.
Let me state, "You can't stop my mission, no matter the
forces that await..."

PART IV: MOTIVATION

Aspire

Motivated with aspirations.
Never clueless, only clued in with no moderation.
Perspectives inspired by new foundations.
No reservations, but the misled need to be fed.
The helplessness is transparent, this is apparent.
All that's needed to be said.

However, to those that think they're too clever:
there's more than meets the eye, far from never.
The land where positivity runs free and the pessimistic mindsets get trapped
through speed.

Planted seeds that grow an inch then die through freeze.
Please, do not bend your curiosity.
Enlarge your ideology to a place where hesitation is lost at sea.

Define that strength that moves mountains as big as the Himalayas and flies
through space like the rockets, see.
This is creed, passion and heart overcoming all odds of defeat.
Sheer strength in the person you see in the mirror as those eyes glare, signs of
no fear.
Channel that inner tiger, lion or cub.
Regardless of the size, you can lift more than a shrub.

Connected

We are connected to the world.
Individually, we're monsters.
We've got potential for anything we feel for, just as long as we feel for it.
Don't let it be misconstrued.
The achievements we plan to reach don't even hit the highest peak that we
currently seek.
Realistic goals push through for what we know and step out of our comfort
zone, grown.
Let us come home and believe in ourselves, as long as we got this wealth and
our health.
Discover the thrills, wander the hills and seek the blissful places that are
necessary stills of life.
They shape the way you think at night and help you develop your hopeful life.

Strike, no pins, we've been handling so many things since school began.
This is the game plan.
The sport of life doesn't give freebies.
We need to come out as one and win like we're only the sixth seed.
Rising to the top, be free but conquering all Kings, they do bleed.
Don't get discouraged by the slips and cracks.
I fell countless times, but still bounced back.
Don't react as if you're under the helm of a whip for that.
Have as much passion as Christ while getting hit, no splat.

Check hazards, we have hard hats.
Listen to the cats that speak recklessly, aristocrats.
No diplomat but a hellraiser.
Keep slicing away, no razor.
Stay motivated; dedicated with hard work.
You are your own savior.

Dreams

Dreams fly as we think about the extraordinary.
Flying and looping to places we've never seen.
We are keen to move up without strangers.
We are all human, making ourselves our own saviors.
Anything you want requires many factors.
We're fishing with no scales, riding different tractors.
Planting seeds, not thinking about the rapture.
To capture all that is needed in your life requires one thing.
Drive!

Elite

You can never be too motivated.
Others around might try to stifle your engagement.
This is where patience becomes practice.
No antics, just tactics.
Dumb down the semantics.
Let them be frantic.
This is gigantic thinking, no sinking, we stay swimming.
Treading above water as they keep skimming.
We are scheming, trying to develop context from the nonsense that gets thrown
our way.
But, forget what you heard, smile and pray.
Your days are brighter than the Sun staring back at you, miles away.
Sit back, relax, and kick your feet up.
Your treat is watching them hit your wall that's stronger than concrete.
Watch them from the rearview, far from the backseat.
They're specs on a sheet.
While you're climbing with cleats, they're watching you from the bottom.
Exclaiming, you're an elite.
It's pretty neat.

Graceland

I fell from grace and I landed on land.
Got up on my feet and hit the button, not to retreat.
But that's why we are unique.
I did not let the situation control me.
I brushed off my shoulder, but let it scold me.
It's a reminder of the times that we've been through and the struggles that were.
We battled through the trenches and got the worst taste but yet, we rose and
faced.
It's a reflection of how you see yourself when your motivation is misplaced.
We race for that finish line usually out of touch like space, but we are forever
striving.
As we tie loose ends, this is life's shoelace.
We commemorate the time by paying homage.
It's the acknowledgment of the 10-year challenge.
Salvage what is necessary and collect your thoughts.
Muster up your courage and continue to get across.
The bridge is the hurdle to overcome like a boss.
Your will should be hotter than tabasco sauce.
Relish your history and clap for progress.
You are your mission.
Enjoy the process.

Heavy Hand

A toast to accolades achieved from elementary school to university.
I see where I came from and patted myself on the back.
The only reason is because I got more scars from the bars that got swung on me.
Bullied from a peewee til' I got right.
My mind started to fight back, all bite.
No bark, just a heavy hand as the man was driven like it was all heart.
Confidence was imperative for me to dictate this narrative.
Many can relate, it's comparative.
A young man finding himself.
Gaining experiences that will carve his mind as tools were dealt.
No felt tip but a razor-sharp point like a joint venture fallen apart.
The collaboration was met with disappointment from the flow chart.
As if one needed a kickstart?
That's how the pendulum swings sometimes and if it does, be combat ready like a buzz.
No peach fuzz, all shaven.
Lined up like the barber was cutting here, no maven.
This is the reason we need to stand up for ourselves.
If you don't do it, do you think other people are coming to help?
Perhaps, but not always.
Learn to stand your ground as if that fight were about to go down.

Invest

Got to invest in yourself.
If you won't, don't expect anyone else to.
It's crucial that you refute downplay.
Many people you meet through all walks of life will leave imprints in some way.
Some will discourage, others will give hope.
But the mindset should be stuck afloat.
No gloat, start, no stroke.
The heart pumps blood that goes for miles.
Let's get back to these files.
It won't do you any good if it's lost like you can't cope.

Find your passion and get your fix, no smack dealer can insist.
This is a reality check you can't cash in.
It's a long-term investment like property wins.
Less glamorous, more intricate, it's different.
The interest will rise as the stock dividends pay out.
The rates you get will determine how you continue to lay the route.
Focus on the finance and budget well.
Set yourself up for retirement before you decide to dwell.
Sell your dreams to yourself and believe.
Only then, will you, succeed.

Staying on Course

Found the entrance that heaven sent.
Searched all about it until I hit my arrogance.
Love the path, I'm living it.
The rise to the top, not stopping it.
Dropping it?
Never heard the phrase since I bought that whole, no layaway.

New move is to go clean, less fiending.
Distract my mind from the bad habits that keep getting opened up like seams.
Dreams and desires to keep on this stream.
Swimming to the deep end with the motion of floating on top is the goal for
eternity.

Challengers presented as gifts.
Don't be distracted from the skills that drift from person to person.
Your strength is in your individuality.
But manage those expectations as that alone can cause severe limitations.
Preparation is key.
Chest out, chin high, like the mindset is beyond belief.

The Great Dash

Waking up every day motivated, starting the jump in a great way.
Mind made up; no decision is grey.
Spot on like the centerpiece, riding into the sunset like it was a good day.
Cuban spot, a cold beverage, not hot.
Living fast, ready to press go, not finishing last.
Haul ass.
The goals and plans scripted for your reference that needs to be pushed pass.
New way of living, I'm reborn.
New transition like ambition is formed.
Every day you get a list of things to do.
By smiling, waking up only gets you on the move.
Prowl til' you get your tools and use them to get to the finish line.
Completed projects exempt from school.
Handling, multitasking at unimaginable feats.
Created to eat, not stressed to beat, but laying it down like a religious greet.
Carrying on at speeds rivaling Santa.
No reindeer like Rudolph with the red nose needed to steer.
Fear has escaped me.
I'm left with the right mindset, that's courage, it's shaped free.

Trials and Tribulations

Trials and tribulations.
It's the very thing that gets people's perspectives in different situations.
Attention is key, observation is free.
Stop and scan, it's the only way you're going to know if you can attain.
Plan for the worst and expect it.
Until then, you can never get settled, can't regret it.
Select it, no DJ, but spinning records for the record is freebase.

Why not go for your dreams?
Take that risk that you wanted to before all those bills started piling up like
leaves.
Manage and budget, be wise.
Don't splurge when it's not necessary to feel the hit if it doesn't work out
perfectly like a well fitted clip.
Smarten up and work those punches.
Don't get caught sleeping as the rest get fit doing crunches.
These are the thoughts of the ones that have heart.
Blood, sweat and tears, overcoming all fears.
Take chances, make mistakes and for God's sakes,
manage high stakes.

Vision

What can I do to make people happy around me?
Do it correctly, don't slip up.
The second you do, these people don't give it up.
But what's the point of trying then?
It sounds like people don't want you to win.

I agree yet disagree.
It was always on me to walk in a straight line sensibly.
Heavy outcomes, narrow minds.
I try to broaden their vision but they're stuck in their own kind.
Fine, I keep trying but there's no luck.
All there is, is my passion and I one day want to live.

Follow your struggles to refuse to work down.
Get in a mindset to achieve greater than the discouraging powers that be
around.
Lost and found, ups and downs.
Maintain the foresight to see obstacles come to light, mustering up your
strength to fight.
Not hype but using all of your might.

There's a difference between defeat and victory.
Your vision, your site.

PART V: LOVE

Bright Future

Walking in the distance and seeing her glide.
Having that feeling deep inside, that I need to talk to this woman and finally realize.
My eyes have not played tricks on me and that's why we are here today.

Understanding the common conception, life is a lesson.
What better way to get through it then with you as my companion?
We are a championship team and we rise together but never fall in between.
We are up like caffeine and as I dream, you are envisioned as my queen.

Her smile is contagious.
Communication, courageous.
Trust like falling backwards without worry.
I hurry for this day to come and as I line up that ring with your finger, those first day thoughts linger.

Will I be able to do this forever and my answer is secured, it's forever!
Holding each other down no matter what and keeping in perspective, we are so tough.
Love is rough, but passion and commitment isn't the small stuff.

This energy is divine, blessed to be surrounded by family that's combined.
This is our journey, forever aligned.

Couples Therapy

Insecurities build as every relationship you had, became still.
Relationship goals are still underway as millions of people cross one another every single day.
What happens when you lose yourself to the woman of your dreams?
For you to get lost in the sense of the scent that was visually seen.
That admiration was as if you're looking up at the queen, but things change like an epiphany.
Symphonies and orchestras playing in your mind.
Think about the shine, smile and laughter.
It's clear you're in the game, not sitting in the rafters waiting for things to change.
You can dictate as much as possible as long as both sides are practical or compromise, not just tactical.
This is rational thinking.
The concept is not preposterous when you're focused on the end game, winning.
Winning? What exactly at?
Life with a spouse, enjoying daily counts in your house and the feeling of, we got here together my dear.
What's crazy about the in between, is all the things the public doesn't see.
The arguing, grueling, nagging, and cracking.
It happens, human nature.
Not farfetched like a flying savior but the inclination for power is greater unless both understand, compassion is only one layer.
Multiple degrees, no separation.
They say we live in the 6.
I say we live and continue to lay down these bricks.
This house will not fall.
Built from the strongest resources in the world, let's use them all.
These prayers are certainly some cannot bear.
But the conception is fair and that would be the creation, rare.
Thus, we are here.

(continued)

A beautiful time lapse of all those that got in the way, simply fade.
What matters most is why we're standing here today.
Love and care-filled emotions.
Even the nonsensical banter is shared through laughter.
It's a perfect thing to see, witnessing what that's like would be an ultimate dream.
No schemes, just the tilt of the head followed with the twinkle in her eyes.
And now, the bite of the tip.
Let's save this for the next session.
Confessions of the lips.

Cuffing Season

I woke up to the scent of you.
I followed my nose all the way through and it led me to the kitchen room.
Where you were there cooking up a hot plate for two.
As you smirk and give me those, "I can eat those eyes."
No lies, but the plate must've been filled with more than just food.
Smiling from a distance, I slid closer.
She pulled me in and pulled the old, pull over.
I am sober, but intoxicated from the twinkle in the eyes.
A bite of the lip and I will stop time.
Let's ride this wave, gripping the two and parting away.
Stay close and I say, let me be your valentine forever and for always, to lay.

Date Night

Beautiful and sweet.
Picked up some flowers, the scent was neat.
Thought about date night, had to find something to eat.
Greetings exchanged with a kiss, that's a delicious treat.

She's getting dolled up, feeling nervous but excited.
Makeup on her face like distinguished features.
One of a kind, passionate about children, she's a teacher.
She's proving worthy, I need to reach her.
She is beyond comfort, far from preacher.

The fluidity of her smile enlarges my heart.
Warm thoughts of the start, even when we race like playing Mario kart.
Smart is an understatement, independent and true.
She makes me complete and we continue to grow all the way through.

Flawless

Beautiful, confident, and free.
Her smile is elegant, beyond that of the sea.
Her vibrant personality runs deep.
More of it than meets the eye.
The power is far from seen.
We are keen to make up but no stranger.
The grace lies in the strut of her heels as she glides.
Seemingly effortless as she brightens up the room.
Acknowledging everyone followed by the scent of her perfume.
Lush hair and thick eyes.
The accentuation is mesmerized.
Only I can say for certainty, she is flawless in her entirety.

Paradise

All I want is you.
I want to set this pace and groove.
As we spoon, I'm bringing you more than a fork.
Ready to eat your food.
This is not crude behavior like intentions of a player.
This is more of an oasis like beach side at the Mediterranean Sea.
I see you rolling your head back and grabbing that hair like you're combing it
for me.
Oh my, you are all that I need.
One look into your soul & I'm filled with glee.
Goodness, gracious, me.

Perfect Ruin

She was beautiful, living stress free.
That's the way I wanted to be and that's the girl I wanted to see.
She's fine in every way.
From her head to her toes, she's well equipped every day.
But it was hard for me to muster up my courage.

I felt weak, as if I didn't have enough porridge.
But I shook it off and approached this star.
It was my spleen that seized up like a fiend who didn't get his fix like sheen.
It was crazy but I still spoke when I saw, standing there felt like a dream.
She was perfect, a beauty queen.

Opened my mouth and a blank stare, frozen.
Time stood still, as if death was in the air.
Sweating in disbelief.
She glares and perks up her eyebrow in despair.
The one chance I had and I let it slip away, rare.

God, give me some luck and let her fall into my lap, like a chair.
Excited from daydreaming, it was clear.
I was just not ready to steer.

Spark Heavy

The curves, I know.
The hair shimmers down as long as it grows.
The skin is smooth and shines as much as it glows.
She dips it down low.
Pops back and forth until she hits the spot where she can't contain herself and
has to let go.
The flow, heavy as it wants to be.
One lucky person gets the treat, it's like a symphony.
A thousand sounds coming together in sparks.
This is electricity.

Tour

I know what you've been going through.
I've been feeling it to.
We see each other everywhere like faces on the moon.
Remember the days we used to use the same spoon.
Just us two.
Laughing and smiling like we just won, it was all in the name of fun.
Alas, I pass into cherished memories of a time when what we had was free.
No fee required, just a small token.
Blossoming into a spectacular sight, no sore eyes or glasses needed to enhance
that prize.
Jeez, it's crazy out there.
Every memory made it clear; we are here.
Sit back, you're secure.
Enjoy this while it lasts.
Your last tour.

True Love

You know it's real when you sit across the table from that special person.
Staring without, talking or blinking twice.
Reminiscing on the things that steered you towards without thinking twice.
This is the height that you have never feared.
Climbing up Mount Everest without gear.
Finding that perfect match to compliment your soul is bold.
Sharing your time, mind and growth.
Happiness uncovered, never before told.
The inclination of this relationship is what was sold.
Bought to be kept for all of time, growing old is just a pastime.
We see it greatly; gravitating towards that aurora of shine is crazy.
Lately, we've been aware of how these two came together without despair.
Understanding, commitment is everywhere.
Two separate stories now combined.
Let's see this journey continue to achieve peaks just as high as your love takes
you.

We

She loves me like never before.
I scored.
Intended to play the short game but handed the long stretch.
She reeled me in, I must confess.
As I rest deep in thought, not a trickle of stress.
I am blessed.
No running around in this field.
I scored the touchdown pass and celebrated with the real.
As happy as can be.
A fight here and there but together WE are WE.
In essence, WE are free.
Long lasting as the seasons end, never agrees.

PART VI: EXPERIENCE

Affection

The cold got colder.
The heart froze over.
Anger with passion that just couldn't work.
My God.
Think about what life could've been had we never went berserk.
Keeping ourselves busy, trying to forget the times spent on something so petty.
Really, we had enough.
Needed to part ways like cargo from a truck.
This is some luck.
Even though it didn't work, let's label this one that struck.
A voltage of charge that gave a lesson.
Once you get hit, get back up and see it lessen.
Good reverend, we need to pray.
Every day is a present and each opportunity presents a question.
Are you willing to take that step and try?
Otherwise, have you really lived or are you just ready to die?

Check

This is God's plan.
Look at your palms, God's hands.
Run and look up, that's a sky scan.
We can be all we want to be.
As long as the passion is pure, and it's connected together like electricity.
As we walk the path towards the goals of our desires.
We stay up; keep ya' head up, 2pac inspired.
Keeping that fire going, full-blown exposure.
No odor, but we can smell that dish.
Feeling like the handouts come back with flips.
Now you owe me X, Y, & Z.
Really?
We had to do this and that.
All we got back is; are you going to pay me?
Understandably complex, full out conversation via text.
What's next? Praying through virtual reality churches?
Heavenly regrets.

False Judgments

They look at you side-eyed comfortably.
The judgment they speak wanders like the company you keep around humbly.
People realize that certain judgments they carry find ways to segregate.
Isn't that scary?
That determines how you're perceived.
I have no reason to fast; things they do, like shoot first, and ask questions last?
It's a rash, a feeling of itch.
Something that you completely want off your skin.
Let us not sin but keep on a high note.
I see those snakes in the grass with a wide scope.
All hope, no glory.
I cherish the days that were initially for me until I saw the deception, it was
clear.
Sometimes, there are no exceptions.
Simple perceptions here.

Gaze

Saw the greatest image in my life.
Got out the concrete jungle into the woods and lost the light.
Pollution shielding us from the natural sights that lit up the sky at night.
Trapped?
Never until I witnessed a glorious canvas that was not on the floor.
I scored.
No door necessary.
All I did was drive into total darkness and looked up.
I finally saw our Milky Way which, only some can say.
Imagine the numerous wonders of outer space.
Shocked as I try to speak but all you hear is stutter.
This is crazy, like my past lover.
Except this one, I won't suffer.

Hustle

Doubt that accompanies fear.
While you don't understand, there are many who stand up as one band and shut down here.
Nervous is what's coming back, and you can't move fast.
You're last, that's just the past time.
I see the struggle and that's my last sign.
I can't get to that place with so much on the damn line.
Every day is a grind.
Achievements go far beyond my gaze and so I reach within deep and come out a simplistic phase.
Realistic, with a hint of craze.
Passionate about the fix I get from this and still I reach for more.
Not greedy, but worth the work.
No body, mind or soul can get me to my knees.
As long as every breath within is a burning desire to fire like a dragon's sneeze.
Freeze up or heat the ground, move like you're walking on hot coals and get those rounds.
Soundwaves and sonar hits.
As the awareness rises and perks up like tips.
No flipping off but high thumbs and the positivity persists.
The secret is out, let's not reminisce.

Jealousy

Lately the shit I've seen, made me beware in the open air that life's a game.
Let's all share through this open lane.
Not understanding this open stain.
Everyone can see the jealousy in the eyes of the ones who aren't wise and can't be unveiled.
Satisfied tails that make you the center of attention and make you want to bail.

Despite this feeling, emotions are stealing.
They can't be controlled like the start of the healing process.
But minds are fragile.
Infinite thinking stretched for a while and can't be stopped or tamed in the wild.
Envy, struggles are empty.
Looking lost like a child in the mall looking for his parents but can't see them at all.
And that's how it begins.
Recognize the feeling long before it ascends into the sky, fleeing without saying bye.

Take advantage, look at the information, take a different vacation, it's a new sensation.
Move past the jealousy, looking at the entirety of this economy and push for what you want.
Develop your needs through this open go and let it be known, blown, and figured out.
The shit you get from this will emerge as the best way out.

Life Lesson

Life is a fickle thing.
You dream large and come out of a small thing.
Bright lights up above; people around trying to round them up.
Growing from a young child to a true man.
Tried to do it all with just a motivational hand.
No bands, just one man.
An army heart stands by the gun hand.
The trigger finger is ready, getting better by bigger and feeling heavy already.

What goes up must come down, but that can be squashed when you hit the top
and refuse to work down.
Frowns all around trying to pull you down but keep fighting and work hard.
No body, minds or soul will rip you apart.

Indian but far from it.
I'm a mix of things like a recipe, you start with it.
Develop into yourself and understand the motion, we are floating on top like
we're boating.
Never showing but overthrowing and coming back with a hole in one.
Like a true champ, we are the chosen ones.

Every experience sheds some light onto your quest or to a place where diligent
minds take flight.
Maybe a fight or two before they rest, good night.
I'm moving in a new direction in life and need to mature fast, snipe.
Wesley got nothing on this blade, it's life's sharp edge, call
it the switch blade.
We're getting paid but stay grinding until we lay down in the earth, family in
dismay.
Disbelief, desire to succeed and feed my family with more than one tree.
Everlasting stand, I'm not moving an inch.
I'm like a statue. Damn.

Mental Pollution

Clouded memories with anger and jealousy.
The passion is against those who get the job done, adding to their legacy.
No holds bar, kick to the gut like a pedigree.
All flash, no substance but wait, an epiphany.
Change in direction, my perfection is to be free from my lapse in capacity.
Actually, letting someone live in your mind rent free is foolish enough.
Let's glide as we slide and send the eviction notice.
Say farewell with a bouquet of Lotus.
Hopeful, what a turn.
Now we rave about the days that we needed to learn.
Clearing up the clouded mind with proper ventilation.
No more hazards as our mentality has changed.
No more pollution in our memory lane.

New Chapter

I'm moving on to the next phase in life.
While I was on a rift, I grabbed that raft and started to drift towards the
shorelines and roped myself in.
Got off the boat and thought:
Was I stuck in the middle afloat for far too long?
Gone too far to do anymore scenes, I saw the signs.
I'm on a new grind, just to finally find my shine and light up.
Smoke to the accomplishments I've reached.
But I'm not done peaking at the height of what I'm really seeking.
Suited up and polished down.
I brush my shoulders off and I'm on the go.
Property just got intellectual and I'm living properly but continue to drive.
The course I've aced has hardly set in and still I thrive.

Perks of Life

Perks of life - Waking up every day.
Perks of life – Being able to walk around and use all of your limbs.
Perks of life – Being able to see, every morning.
Perk of life - Enjoying the sun rays as it hits your top.
Perks of life - Being able to see your parents every day.
Perks of life - Being able to eat.
Perks of life - Having friends.
Perks of life - Having family.
Perks of life – Having your own free will.
And finally,
Life - the perk itself.

Striking Lines

I'm moving in a new direction.
Keep your discretion and feel for inception.
A new way of corrections.
Misconception got me looking lost like I fell from the sky and hit the ground
soft.
Now I'm heading to my spot, dreading what awaits in my neighbourhood, those
are cops.
They roll around; they're on the city's payroll so they roll around town.
But they're bloodhounds, shooting innocent people like they're pure evil.
Real troops get in the line of fire like upheaval.

See, the fruits of our labour go unnoticed.
Only when something bad happens, we have giant lights flashing down as it's
focused.
No lotus, but a green leaf.
I see the politics suck the life out of those who feel their beliefs.
Race wars continuing fast, while the furious protest, the political powers never
confess.
Nonetheless, city officials always try to compress those below the poverty line
like that was always the plan, so don't stress.
We're still waiting patiently for this city to change with positive progress.
But we continually see those dark shadows oppress.

Let us come together like a conquest and fight hard to win.
Overpowering congress.

Viral Gor, popularly known as VIRUS THE POET, is an internationally recognized Canadian poet and author. He gained fame through his captivating poetry collection, Poetry is Motion: Mind, Body & Soul, an international best seller.

As a seasoned performer, Viral travels across the globe, captivating audiences on prestigious stages in Paris, London, Toronto, NYC, San Francisco, Miami and many more. One of his notable achievements includes receiving a national award for his exceptional poem titled "Home." This remarkable piece of literature was later published by the esteemed Poetry Institute of Canada, further solidifying his reputation as a distinguished poet. Viral's poetry transcends cultural boundaries, delving into universal themes that resonate deeply with his readers worldwide.

Connect with VIRUS THE POET:

https://www.virusthepoet.com
https://www.instagram.com/virusthepoet
https://www.twitter.com/VirusthePoet
https://www.facebook.com/virusthepoet